HOW TO R...

A veteran occultist explains several ways by which auric sight may be developed. Techniques of etheric healing are given, and the author also explains the colours of the aura, etheric leakage, psychic vampirism, and how to re-charge one's etheric 'batteries'.

HOW TO READ
THE AURA

by

W.E. Butler

THE AQUARIAN PRESS

First published 1971
Second Edition, revised, enlarged and reset, 1979

ISBN 0-85030-179-3

*The Aquarian Press is part of the Thorsons Publishing Group,
Wellingborough, Northamptonshire, NN8 2RQ, England*

Printed in Great Britain by
William Collins Sons & Co. Ltd., Glasgow

9   11   13   15   17   16   14   12   10

CONTENTS

CHAPTER ONE

WHAT IS THE AURA?

Following my usual custom, I propose to define as well as I can what the aura is. Those of you who have read my other books will have noticed that I usually give the ordinary dictionary definition of the subject, and I do this because it establishes a common ground between my readers and myself.

According to my dictionary, therefore, the aura is defined as 'a subtle invisible essence or fluid said to emanate from human and animal bodies, and even from things; a psychic electro-vital, electro-mental effluvium, partaking of both mind and body, hence the atmosphere surrounding a person; character; personality. In a pathological sense meaning a premonitory symptom of epilepsy and hysteria'.

I think we may ignore the second part of this definition, though I suppose many would say that anyone who claims to see the aura must himself be subject to hysteria, if to nothing worse! However, as we go on with this study of the aura, I hope you will be reassured, and will not feel that you are being led into hysterical ways of thought and feeling.

Luminous Atmosphere

The aura is usually seen as a luminous atmosphere around all living things, including what it used to be the custom to regard as inanimate matter. Advancing knowledge begins to suggest to the scientist that even in this so-called 'dead' matter there are living forces at work, thus supporting the old Persian poet who wrote of Life as 'sleeping in the mineral, dreaming in the plant, awakening in the animal and becoming conscious of itself in man'.

In many stained glass windows we see representations of Christ and His Apostles in which the aura is portrayed as a surround of golden light. In many cases we only get the nimbus or radiance shown around the head of the figure, but in others it surrounds the whole form.

The same pictorial convention is also found in some Buddhist paintings of a very early date. This may of course, be due in this case to the far-reaching influence of the early Nestorian Christian Church, which sent out its missionaries throughout the whole of the East, though to offset this it is to be noted that this same way of expressing the spirituality of the person portrayed is to be found in early Hindu and Persian art. A simple explanation may be that the artists who originated this conventional way of indicating the moral structure of certain people were themselves able to see this strange phenomenon which has been termed the 'aura'.

False Auras

The appearance of what seems to be a luminous atmosphere surrounding people has been reported by a very great number of people down the ages. In less critical ages such an aura of light was thought to be a sign of spiritual advancement, but in more modern times it is usually dismissed as either a figment of the imagination or an indication of either mental instability or optical disease. There is some justification for this latter view that disease of the eye is responsible for such appearances of light around a person, and there is one common cause of illusion in this connection.

It often happens that someone in an audience will remark of a speaker to whom he has been listening intently, that his aura was quite perceptible to him. In some cases this may actually have been the case, but often the cause is a purely physical one and has nothing whatever to do with this radiating influence which we call the aura.

The explanation is fairly simple. If one gazes with fixed attention at someone for a lengthy period of time, as, for instance when one is listening to a lecture, the muscles controlling the focusing mechanism of the eyes become fatigued, and the eye-focus suddenly alters. When this happens, the new image which is being received upon the retina falls on a slightly different point, and the result is that the old image is seen as a 'surround' to the one we are looking at. This surround will be in the *complementary* colours to that of the person, and will usually be seen as a white or yellow band of light around him. This is purely a physiological phenomenon, but in an exceedingly large number of cases it is taken to be a vision of the aura.

It is important that anyone who is attempting to develop and train extra-sensory perceptions should start by cultivating the most scrupulous honesty. It is far too easy to drift into a slack and easy dishonesty, and to give vague and sketchy descriptions carefully, though often unconsciously, formulated in such a way as to take advantage of a lack of the critical faculty in those to whom the description is given. Or, in the words of an American slang term, you 'bunco steer' the person concerned to believe what you have deduced he wants to believe. This is a very real trap for the unwary and the best remedy to prevent oneself from falling into it is to adopt a high standard of honesty.

This standard is rewarding, for it enables us to trust our vision when we have begun to use it, and this certainty is a valuable thing.

The Field of Force

If we accept the definition which the dictionary gives, we see it refers to a 'psychic electro-vital and electro-mental effluvium'. Let us see just what this means. It is now well established that all the activities of our physical body are associated with electric currents which circulate throughout the organs, and which actually form a definite electrical 'field' around us. Russian scientists have recently perfected apparatus which, they claim, can detect this very faint field of force which exists around all living things. They have claimed to detect the presence of such fields extending some twenty-five centimetres from the bodies of some insects.

Incidentally, this field of force has nothing at all to do with the electrical 'charge' which some young ladies acquire by wearing nylon dresses or using nylon bed sheets. The charge of static electricity which is often built up by friction against such material can give quite a smart shock. A mild form of this may be seen if a nylon garment is taken off in the dark when the air is dry. The charge is released in a crackling shower of small sparks. This, however, is quite different to the 'biological electricity' which is linked with all our bodily activities. So we have in and around us an electrical 'field of force' which may be considered as the first and most dense of the several such fields of force which make up the composite emanation which we call the 'aura'.

Although the term is one which is objected to by those who have had training as physicists, there is a name already in use which we may use, and this is the 'etheric aura'. There is, of course, a still denser aura which is composed of the minute solid particles which are being constantly thrown off from the physical body itself. Such minute particles are left by us upon everything we touch, and go to make up the 'scent' by means of which we can be tracked by a dog or other animal. We have of late years been made acutely conscious of this by numerous advertisements relating to what is discreetly referred to as 'B.O.' We refer to it here in order to cover the physical aspect of the aura, since these particles also carry with them something of the tenuous substance which is constantly being thrown out from a much finer 'body' than this 'too, too solid flesh' which so many of us regard as the only body we possess.

The True Physical Body
Those who have studied these matters have become convinced, by direct experience in many cases, that we possess a finer body which, although still a *physical* body, is of an extremely ethereal and tenuous nature. Certain schools of thought refer to this finer physical substance as 'pre-matter', and in

old occult writings it was referred to as the 'astral' substance. In modern occultism that name has been transferred to another type of substance, and this often causes confusion when people read some of the old books and try to understand them under the new descriptions.

Now this ethereal body is the *true* physical body (it persists from our birth until our death) whereas the coarser dense matter which we usually think of as our material body constantly changes. It has been said that every molecule of our body is changed for a new one within three years, so that there is a constant flow of material particles from this physical body, and a constant replacement by new particles as the forces of what is called 'metabolism' work within us.

'Katabolic' and 'Anabolic' Metabolism

Metabolism is operating in us in two opposite ways. As the 'katabolic force' it breaks down the very complex chemical compounds of our bodies into simpler forms and these are expelled from the body. As the 'anabolic force' it builds up from simpler compounds supplied by our food and drink the highly complex compounds which replace those already broken down and eliminated.

Thus there is a cycle of breaking down and building-up constantly in progress within us. Varying rates and ratios of this metabolic process result in varying conditions of the physical body, and it is one of the chief teachings of occultism that the metabolic processes are initiated from and controlled by the 'body' of finer pre-matter which we term the 'etheric body'.

This finer body has received various names. Amongst the Egyptians of old, it was known as the *Ka*, and in medieval Europe as the *Doppelganger*. In the East it has been known as the *'Linga Sharirah'* in French Spiritism as the *'Perisprit'* and in various old writings it was known as the 'astral body' or 'double'. In certain Rosicrucian schools it is called the 'Vital Body', and this brings us to its particular significance in our study of the aura.

The Etheric Aura

Occultists claim that, as well as controlling the intake and egress of physical material from the body, the etheric body also draws vital energy, or *Prana*, from the sun and other forms of energy from the earth itself, for use in the living economy of the body cells. These energies circulate throughout the etheric body and its dense material counterpart, and having supplied the needs of the organism, they are radiated out from the etheric body in a peculiar haze which extends all round the body for some inches beyond its surface.

This haze, which is usually the first part of the aura to be seen, is known as the *etheric aura*. Since the etheric body is so closely connected with all the vital processes of the body, the appearance which the etheric aura presents is usually a good guide to the physical health of the person concerned, and the practice of diagnosis by the aura is one which is widespread in occult circles.

I have said that we have more than one 'body', and we have just been considering the etheric body. Now we come to other bodies, and here the term 'body' becomes somewhat misleading. We usually

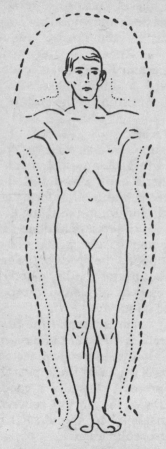

Male aura

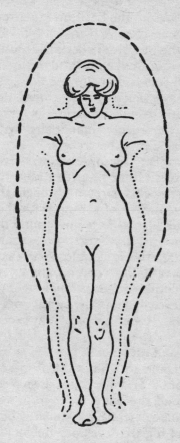

Female aura

think of a body in terms of the one body with which we are familiar, our dense physical one, but these finer bodies are best described as 'vehicles' or 'sheaths'. In fact, in the East this latter term is used, and they are known as *Koshas*.

Now it is the practice in certain occult schools to refer to the 'emotional body' and the 'mental body', and although this is correct from one point of view, I think we may safely say that seldom indeed do we think without some admixture of emotion, and seldom do we react emotionally without *some* thought entering into the process.

The two aspects of consciousness, emotion and mind, are closely linked together, and the energies of the inner worlds stream through the 'bodies' which are our means of contact with those worlds. These energies also radiate out around the physical body, but over a far larger area than the vital energies of the etheric double. Whereas the extent of those vital radiations can usually be reckoned in inches, the combined emotional-mental radiation extends for several feet in the average person, and in more highly developed people it may exceed this.

The Spiritual Aura

Finally, we come to what we may describe as the 'spiritual aura', and here the area over which it extends beyond the body varies from a few feet, in the case of unevolved people to yards or even miles in the case of highly developed people. It is said in the East that the spiritual aura of the Lord Gautama Buddha extended for two hundred miles, and they also say that the whole of this planet is held in the aura of a very great Being. This is also

Christian teaching, though it is usually restricted to the presence of Deity: 'In Him we live and move and have our being', as St Paul says.

It will be clear, from what I have said, that there is not one aura, but several auras, each with its own peculiarities, working together as a composite atmosphere surrounding us, and being part of the flow of inner energies through all parts of our being. It will also be evident that each level of this aura can only be discerned by an appropriate mode of perception or vision.

Emanations

Those of my readers to whom this idea of emotional and mental 'bodies' may be somewhat difficult may disregard it for all practical purposes, since, as I have said, these two aspects of consciousness almost always work together in the ordinary person. Nevertheless, the testimony of many clairvoyants is that these bodies or vehicles of consciousness do actually exist. However, they may be disregarded, and attention fixed upon the emanations which stream out beyond the limits of the physical body when we are recording, as we always are, the impressions which are being received in consciousness from the workings of the senses, both physical and superphysical.

Even in states of what we think of as 'unconsciousness', i.e., in trance, sleep or pathological states due to disease, accident, drug-taking and so on, the aura is still actively engaged in responding to those impressions which are being received from the subconscious levels of our mind, and that part of the aura which we have referred to as the 'etheric aura' still shows the fluctuations of the vital forces of the body.

Also, and this is important, the aura is at all times registering the general emotional and mental quality of our consciousness, and this general quality is something which is relatively stable, and is, indeed due to a long-continued series of emotional and mental habits of the conscious mind.

The result is to give to the aura a certain general colouring which changes comparatively slowly. This basic colouring gives to the clairvoyant a clear indication of the emotional, mental and spiritual character of its owner. This point will be dealt with more fully when I come to the interpretation of the various appearances which are presented to the seer by the action of thought and emotion on the aura.

In the next chapter I want to consider the structure of the aura, since this will give some insight into its character and help you to understand the important part which it plays in ordinary life.

CHAPTER TWO

THE STRUCTURE OF THE AURA

It must be kept in mind that the aura has two definite apects. There is what we may call the 'form' or 'shape' of the aura; the ovoid of coloured emanations which surrounds and interpenetrates the physical body, and the underlying currents of energy which cause it to keep this shape. The latter currents may be considered as a 'magnetic' or 'psychic' field of force, through which the finer substances of the inner levels of manifestation are continually flowing.

The 'Silver Cord'

I have referred in the last chapter to the etheric, emotional and mental emanations which go to make up the totality of the aura, and we may regard these as making up two quite definite constituents thereof. The etheric body is so closely linked with the physical body that we may, for all practical purposes, regard it as the *true* physical body, upon which the gross outer physical form has been moulded. As it influences the physical form which we think of as our body, we could also consider the etheric double to be the 'inner physical body', and the flesh and blood body to be the 'outer physical body'. These two are connected by what is usually termed the 'silver cord', an allusion to that verse in the Bible which says 'Or ever the silver cord be loosened', this being part of a very wonderful statement case in poetical form describing the process of old age and death.

Those who have developed the faculty of clairvoyance claim to be able to see this silver cord if they are observing someone who is dying. Briefly, as death approaches, they see a silvery duplicate form leave the dying body, until it is entirely clear of it except for what seems to be a cord or line of silvery light which connects the two bodies. As long as that cord is intact, there is always the possibility of the consciousness returning to the material body again, but once the cord breaks, the separation is complete, and no such return is possible. The man is 'dead'.

The Etheric Double

At the same time, the denser part of the etheric body is still connected with the dead physical body, for each individual cell of that body has its etheric independent life, and will continue to live in a purely vegetative manner until the conditions become such that it can no longer function in any way. There is much to be learnt concerning the functions exercised by the etheric double, and in these days of 'organ transplants' and the gruesome prospect envisaged by some Russian scientists of idiots being kept alive and used as host bodies to nurture 'transplants' until such spare parts are called for, this is a line of research for those qualified to conduct it which might well be helpful to mankind.

The whole phenomenon of 'rejection', the mechanism by which the body rejects an alien organ, may turn out to be more complex than is at present realized, and factors other than bio-chemical ones may be involved.

Indeed, all medical research could be improved if this etheric double was recognized and steps taken to observe its workings. Under such conditions it might be found possible to dispense with much of vivisectional research, which is often misleading, as certain tragic happenings in connection with the manufacture of drugs have made us aware. Also, freedom from dependence upon questionable experiments would be a moral blessing to those medical men who consider that they must use such research in the best interests of their patients, but who feel nevertheless that the methods of research are morally evil.

Of course, one would not for a moment suppose that the possibility of using such etheric vision as a tool of biological research would be considered by the majority of medical men at the present day. However, if the results of 'etheric research' should prove both more satisfactory and more readily applied, then they would be compelled to fall into line with their more enlightened colleagues. This, of course, is a very 'long-term' idea, but things are moving so rapidly in this present age that it is unwise to set any limits as to what might or might not be done in the near future.

Disease Indicated by Etheric Aura

What we have called the 'etheric aura' is the general radiation, the 'field of force' of the etheric body, and it indicates what the conditions in that body are. Since the etheric directly controls and affects the physical body, it often happens that disease is indicated by the etheric aura long before it becomes evident in the physical and it is in this etheric body that the real remedial action begins. If the indications can be seen in the etheric aura, then it is possible to treat them on that level, and much of the 'faith-healing', psychic and spiritual healing, takes place in this region of the human being. Because of the fact that the etheric aura accurately indicates disease conditions which are either latent in the etheric body or have already begun to manifest on the physical levels, if has often been termed the 'health aura'.

The Dual Etheric Aura

Observations which have been carried out on this health aura have disclosed some very interesting facts. Its general appearance is that of a 'surround' of fine hair-like emanations which form a rough oval around the physical body. The shape of this ovoid often indicates ill-health, by being 'bulgy' or by other departures from the shape taken by the aura of a person in good health. I have referred to this oval of the etheric aura as though it were a simple thing, but further research has shown that so far from being simple in appearance, it is somewhat complex, and some of these complexities are of the greatest interest. The etheric aura of a person is actually dual, comprising an 'outer' and an 'inner' part.

There is an inner aura which follows the general shape of the body, and is about three or four inches (this is somewhat variable) from its surface. Then there is an outer aura which extends to about a foot from the body, though this distance is more variable than in the case of the inner aura. Even this is not the totality of the aura, much finer and less easily detected, which extends far out from the surface of the outer aspect of the general aura. This does not seem to have any definite boundary at all, and it may be due to some action by the organized aura of the individual upon the general etheric atmosphere, in somewhat the same way as an electrified body will induce electrical activity in surrounding objects.

Rays of Light

Another interesting phenomenon connected with the etheric aura is the occasional appearance within it of what seem to be rays or shafts of light which in most cases appear to start from the physical body and then ray out into the space around. In some cases it has been noticed that such rays passed to someone or something near at hand, and it was ascertained that the person whose aura was being studied was, in fact, thinking strongly of that person or object to which the auric ray had gone. It may be that we have here one aspect of a telepathic transmission of feeling and thought. However, I shall try to deal with the question of the role of the aura in telepathy later on in this book.

We come now to another interesting aspect of the aura. This is what is commonly termed the 'dark space'. It is from one-sixteenth to a quarter of an inch in thickness, and exactly follows the outline of the body. All the auras appear to start from this dark space, which I think may be the actual surface of the etheric body itself. Of course, it could be a still further part of the aura, but research has not yet determined the exact part which it plays.

Finally, as I have already said, there is an aura which is due to the biological actions taking place in the body and in the skin. These result in the generation of a minute electro-magnetic field around the physical body, and this can be measured by the use of sensitive instruments. It appears to be increased when strong light falls upon the surface of the body, and different types of light, ultra-violet, infra-red and the primary colours, have varying effects on this field.

The Etheric Skin

So much for the general description of the aura as it is seen by a good clairvoyant, or by the use of the 'Kilner Screens'. Now both the inner and outer auras appear to have what we may think of as a surface skin, and these etheric skins play an important part in the actual health of the individual. When they are observed closely, they are found to be made up of innumerable etheric lines of force, almost as though the ends of the striations or hairlike lines which make up the aura were twisted together to form a covering and protective envelope to the entire aura.

Etheric Leakage

In a normal person in good health, the etheric skin presents an unbroken surface, but for many reasons this is the ideal rather than the actual state of things. In most people there appear to be what can best be described as 'wounds' and 'tears' in it, and these appear to allow for what we may term 'etheric leakage'.

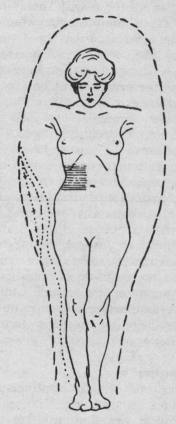

Abnormal shape of aura with gradual recovery.
A dark patch on the right side.

Such open areas in the aura were well known to those who studied these matters in the past, and they called them 'orbicular wounds'. Certain practices in connection with mediumship can, sometimes, cause these orbicular wounds, and for this reason the older occultists were not altogether in favour of the *indiscriminate* development of mediumship. Many of the more thoughtful spiritualists at the present time have come to have the same conclusion in this matter.

Anyway, the orbicular wound was taken seriously by the old occultists, and, I think, with good reason. One of the most serious results of such a 'leaking aura' is that vitality is quickly lost, and the unfortunate person concerned goes through life in a thoroughly devitalized condition, and thus has little energy to attempt any work, and little power to resist the onset of disease.

If the etheric vitality is low, then the metabolism of the body will suffer, and under these circumstances the build-up of 'anti-bodies', which will prevent the onset of disease, is sadly curtailed. So the unfortunate person will succumb to diseases which will only slightly affect his more robust and healthy brother.

Psychic Vampirism

Not only, however, will the vital energy pour out from the aura of one who has sustained the orbicular wound. Its flow can be considerably increased by the 'vampire-action' of certain people who can only maintain a normal amount of vital energy by drawing it continually from others around them. In most cases this psychic vampirism is a purely unconscious happening, and the psychic vampires would be horrified to learn that they were doing this thing. Most of us have met, at one time or another, people who depleted one by their presence. Often they are sincere and dedicated seekers after spiritual truth, but the fact remains that anyone coming into close contact with them for half-an-hour or so leaves feeling that he has been drained of all vitality. (Conversely, the one who has drained him of energy in this way, may be heard to say that they really enjoy a visit from Mr So-and-So, they feel so much better after they have been to visit him!)

Apart, however, from this depletion, there is a corresponding suction, as it were, on their part, as the depleted vital body attempts to re-charge itself. But because of the wound in the auric skin, instead of the new vitality being drawn in through the correct and normal channels, it is drawn in from whatever happens to be around in the way of etheric energy. As the sources of such energy may be neither normal nor desirable, the net result of this may be the re-charging of the body with polluted and undesirable forces, and these may bring with them in their train the conditions which will pre-dispose them to disease.

Etheric Parasites

Also, just as physical sojourn in undesirable places and conditions may cause one to collect parasites of different kinds, such as bugs, fleas and lice, so the undesirable forms of psychic life which exist in physical conditions of dirt and neglect will be picked up and become parasites on the etheric aura, where they may be seen by anyone possessing the slightest degree of clairvoyant power.

These etheric parasites appear to be simple forms of life which, in their own place and under their own normal conditions have a definite part to play in the etheric realm. In this realm there are to be found many grades of living intelligences, as well as a great deal of 'throw-out' psychic material which is ultimately dealt with by the purifying processes which are continually at work in these levels, and is then returned to normal etheric circulation. Here, too, there are great currents of energy which sweep through the whole realm and act upon the physical plane in many subtle ways.

These currents, known in the East as the *Tatvas*, appear to be closely connected with the activity of the sun, and to be somehow concerned with the basic nature of physical matter; that is, its appearance in solid, liquid, gaseous and radiant forms (corresponding to the old alchemical idea of the 'Four Elements' of Earth, Air, Fire, and Water.)

Here in the etheric realm lie the keys to medicine, psychology and psychism, and anyone who submits to the arduous training required to develop and organize his etheric awareness will find a rich field of research which so far has only been explored on a small scale.

Psychedelic Drugs

To return, however, to our consideration of the etheric boundary around the aura. Certain forms of unwise psychic and mediumistic development will cause an orbicular wound, and this can also be the end result of the use of alcohol in excessive quantities, as well as being quite commonly the cause of the mental and emotional deterioration shown by those who have become drug addicts. This is especially the cause with those who have become habitually conditioned to the use of *some* of the so-called 'psychedelic drugs' such as LSD.

Incidentally, this is a realm of action where emotional prejudices are rife, and it is not fair to say that *all* drugs cause mental deterioration. However, for anyone desiring to become psychically aware, and proposing to use these drugs for the purpose, the best advice would be 'DON'T'. This advice certainly holds good where the psychedlic drugs are concerned. There are better ways of expanding consciousness than these, though they take longer to produce the desired effect.

In these days of instant coffee, instant cooking, instant quite a lot of other things, there seems to be a demand for 'instant psychic ability'. In some rare cases, where the psychic make-up of the person is of a certain type, the psychic abilities may be developed in such a short time that in these cases we might speak of instant psychism, but this is not the general rule, and even where it is, the newly developed faculty needs long and careful training before it can be used to the best advantage.

The etheric body is constantly receiving its energy from two sources with which I will deal presently, but it will tend to draw upon the energy of other people if for any reason the vitality pressure is low and there exists this wound in the aura which allows the vital energy to leak away.

Vital Energy

There are people who appear to draw the vital energy from its normal sources in such abundance that, when their own organisms have received all that they need, there is a considerable surplus remaining, and this 'charges' their auras, and rays out as a steady stream of vital energy to all around. Such people are sometimes to be found in the nursing profession, and their mere presence in the room will stimulate the vital forces of their patients. This is vaguely realized by many people, who will say of such a nurse, 'She gives you strength when she is near you'. Others, equally dedicated to healing, produce no such result, for in their case, they seem to be drawing in just sufficient vital energy to supply their own needs.

In another chapter of this book, I will discuss the question of the superabundance of vital energy in certain people in connection with what is known as 'magnetic healing', for here the aura is used in a definite way.

I have referred to the 'vampire' activities of some people, and have pointed out that in many cases such people are quite unaware of the results they produce upon those around them. It will be seen from what I have said that in both the vampire and his victim there is a lack of vital energy. In the vampire type, the etheric aura reaches out, as it were and draws from others the extra energy it requires.

In the victims the lack of vital energy causes what we may describe as a 'vitality vacuum' and they will also tend to draw into their aura any surplus energy which may be available. There are many such sources, some good and some bad, and it is unfortunately the case that as a general rule the person who possesses the orbicular wound, or the 'leaky aura', if you prefer that term, tends to draw extra energy from organized life-units of a lower type, such as certain animals, or from others who are even more negative than themselves, such as very small children. There are much better sources from which they could draw the extra vitality they require, one of which is the etheric aura of living plants, more particularly trees of a certain kind.

A great deal of private research has been carried out into this interesting aspect of the subject, and in the chapter which I have promised you on the whole question of the aura and healing I shall give you some instructions which you may find to be of great use when and if you ever find yourself depleted of vitality.

A Leaky Aura

Of course, in the case of someone who has a leaky aura, the obvious thing to do is to plug up the leak. Unfortunately such a simple solution is seldom thought of, let alone put into practice, possibly because it *is* so very obvious. Instead, vital energy is pumped into the person concerned, only to be lost almost immediately, and a fresh re-charge becomes necessary.

The whole subject of this auric skin or envelope is one which presents fascinating problems for those who desire to understand more of the mysterious way in which our consciousness makes contact with our physical body and brain mechanism.

This area of research also permits the application

of the scientific method of study in a way which is much more difficult in the case of the emotional and mental levels of consciousness.

Be it noted, however, that this etheric aura and the etheric body from which it emanates is strongly affected by personal thought or that of other people, and since the etheric is the controlling level from which the physical is directed, we have here a clue to the success of some metaphysical systems of healing, such as those associated with the New Thought Movement, with the Unity Movement and with Christian Science.

Supernormal Manifestation

Very many carefully controlled experiments in hypnosis, together with the accounts of spontaneous phenomena such as the alleged 'stigmata' (the reproduction of the wounds of Christ which have been seen to appear on the bodies of some Christian Saints; St Francis of Assisi being an example), together with many well authenticated accounts of 'firewalking' and other exploits of some Eastern ascetics, as well as the physical phenomena of spiritualism, all suggest that this etheric body and its aura plays an important part in what is usually termed '*supernatural* manifestation', but which should more correctly be termed '*supernormal* manifestation'.

Without going into the vexed question of the proofs of personal survival, we can at least say that here in this borderland between the physical and the more tenuous levels of the emotional-mental worlds, there is a promising field for the students of psychical research hitherto somewhat neglected.

CHAPTER THREE

THE CIRCUIT OF FORCE

In order to prevent the previous chapter from becoming too long I decided to deal with further aspects of the structure of the aura in this third chapter. I have used the title 'The Circuit of Force' since what I have to say is very largely concerned with the flow of energy through the etheric aura. I have already touched upon one of the pathologies of the aura, the 'leaky aura' or 'auric wound', and I think that what I have to say here may help the reader to see how such a wound may be healed, and, what is better still, how it may be prevented from happening at all.

Established Teachings

First of all, it may be helpful if we consider what this auric energy is, and from whence it is derived. Here we come up against certain established teachings which have in the past been taken very much for granted by many students of occultism; particularly by followers of general theosophical teaching. In some fairly important respects such teaching differs from that given in the western esoteric school, and, for the matter of that, from that given in the eastern esoteric schools. In a way, this is all to the good, for to find the 'authorities' differing may help the enquirer to keep his mind open to new outlooks and teachings.

In the same way, to use the illustration of the

present state of astronomical knowledge, there is a decided difference between the advocates of what is called the 'big bang' theory of the beginning of this universe, and the opposite theory of the 'steady state universe', and the efforts of each side to prove *their* hypothesis to be the correct one are having the effect of rapidly increasing our general knowledge of the universe in many other aspects, entirely apart from its origins.

So, in this difference in the teachings, there is room for independent research, and for this reason, though I shall put forward the general teaching which I have myself received, I shall endeavour to compare it with that given from the other sources of which I have spoken, and in addition will describe some of my own observations in this field. Then those of you who may yourself develop the power to observe the aura will feel free to make your own experiments without worrying about whether your results agree with those recorded by theosophical seers, eastern yogis, spiritualist psychics and mediums or even those personal observations recorded by me in this and other books!

Chakras or 'Centres'

The general occult teaching is that the etheric body draws vitality from the sun and distributes it to the various parts of the body. Another teaching, the western esoteric one, teaches that the etheric body is drawing energy not only from the sun but also from the earth as well. This western teaching, which I consider to be a fuller exposition of what happens in this drawing in of vitality, affirms that there are certain points within the etheric body, all located along the spinal column, through which this dual stream of vitality is passed into the physical body. This is also taught in the other school, but the nature and number of these 'distribution points' or *chakras*, as they are termed in the east, are differently described in the two systems.

In the ordinary theosophical teaching, there are said to be seven of these *chakras* or 'centres', namely, the centre above the head known generally as the 'thousand-petalled lotus', the centre between the eyes, the throat centre, the heart centre, the solar plexus centre, the spleen centre and the sacral centre at the base of the spine.

In the western teaching, the centres are given as the centre above the head, the centre at the throat, the heart centre, the sex centre, the centre below the feet. (In both systems the centre above the head is located in that part of the aura which extends above the head, and in the western system, the centre below the feet is also said to be in that part of the aura which extends downwards below the soles of the feet.)

It will be seen that whereas the general theosophical teaching speaks of *seven* centres, the western system speaks of only *five*. In the eastern tantric system we have the centres as given in the theosophical teaching, with the exception that the spleen centre is not mentioned, and its place is taken by the sex centre.

Occult Work in India

When I was in India, I did a fair amount of practical work in connection with occult matters as a member of a small group of advanced occultists,

and in the teaching I there received, there is, I
think, the answer to this apparent discrepancy
between the systems. We were taught, and it was
demonstrated to us, that there were many such
'centres' in the etheric body, and certain people
tended to concentrate upon some of these and
ignore others. All, it was taught, were part of an
intricate system of etheric channels through which
the life-forces, including the vital force known as
prana, were constantly circulating.

The reasons why certain people tended to use a
'centre' which others apparently did not worry
about were complex, and it was best, so our
mentors said, to find out for oneself which was the
natural combination of centres for us, personally,
and to leave our neighbour to work on his own
combination if he found it of benefit. Further
personal research, together with the reported
findings of many other psychics has confirmed this,
and I would simply advise any of you who may
worry about these differences to work along those
lines and follow those teachings which seem, *to you*,
to be helpful.

Tantric Practices

We were told that the substitution of the spleen
centre for the sex centre in the theosophical
teaching was largely due to a certain unconscious
bias against any inclusion of sexual ideas in the
matter, since, in the case of certain *debased* Tantric
practices, and certain *debased* witch-cult practices
the sexual element had been grossly emphasized.

You will notice that I have italicized the word
'debased'. This is because I once received an

indignant letter accusing me of being unfair when I referred to 'debased Tantric practice' in one of my former books. The trouble was, I had not emphasized the word 'debased', and my critic was under the impression that I was attacking the entire Tantric system, which I most assuredly was not. It is a lofty eastern system of practical philosophy and can no more be blamed for the excesses of *some* practitioners of Tantric magic than can the Christian Churches be blamed for the occasional Black Mass which one hears about, now and then.

Western Classification of Centres

However, to return to our list of 'centres'. The western classification is quite in line with the general theosophical one if the centre above the head is regarded as the one which draws in energy from the sun, and if it is also thought of as being the cause of the lesser centre located between the eyes. The cardiac and solar plexus centres together will then form the centre which is located in that part of the body, and the generative centre can be considered in conjunction with the centre at the base of the spine as one centre.

So we have only lost the spleen centre, and it may be that this particular centre has other functions. It has been observed that in some cases where the etheric body temporarily left the physical, it apparently used the spleen centre as its gate of exit.

We are now reduced to the five centres referred to in the western teaching. I'm sorry if this upsets anyone who feels that the mystic number seven has been thrown into the discard. Personally, I do not feel that there is any mystic virtue in the number seven, at least as far as this subject is concerned, whatever its significance may be in the fields of numerology and symbolism, but, of course, I may be mistaken! If so, then I must ask the reader's pardon.

The centres which are apparently located along the spine appear to extend out to the surface of the aura in what seem to look like cones or trumpet-shaped vortices of energy, and where these vortices touch the outer skin of the aura, they are covered by what looks like a fine and tenuous web of etheric substance. These vortices are constantly in a spinning motion, and according to the direction of their 'spin', so energy appears to be drawn in or directed out.

I have said that in the system which I am now working with, the centre above the head is regarded as drawing energy from the sun, and this energy when so drawn in, charges up the solar plexus centre strongly. But here we come to a difficult point in our observations, and for that reason it would certainly be of the greatest value if other observers were to study the whole question of this vitality intake. The point at issue is, whether this solar energy (which is specialized by the solar plexus centre) is the entire energy intake. Or is it simply a stimulating and 'triggering' charge which causes an increased amount of vital power to be drawn from the great primary current of energy which comes into the etheric from the etheric world itself? If the latter supposition be correct, does this energy arrive by way of the centre which lies below the feet in the aura?

Mental and Emotional Stimulus

In any case, when the solar plexus centre is in action in this way, it distributes its energy to all the other centres. Equally, the head, throat and generative centres appear to be stimulated by certain types of energy which they draw from the etheric levels, quite apart from the general vitality which is distributed to them from the solar plexus.

Here I must touch upon something which is, I think, not sufficiently realized by many who work along occult lines. This is, that these centres can be stimulated into full activity not only by energies from the sun and other sources, but also by mental and emotional stimulus, such as ritual, the cinema and theatre, the television screen or any book which is so written that it builds up clear and well defined images in the mind of its reader and also stimulates the emotions. I feel that this is an important aspect of auric mechanism, and the implications thereof in our lives may be far more powerful than we at present realize.

Wounding the Aura

I have been describing something of what happens as the centres draw in energy. What happens when they reverse their spin and begin to pour out energy? First of all, the fine web over the outside end of the vortices acts as an automatic check upon the amount of energy which may be projected and so prevents the individual losing energy to a dangerous extent. So long as this restraining web is undamaged, this automatic restraint on the vital forces act efficiently, but there are conditions which may arise when it is damaged, and then we have the 'auric wound' of which I have written.

Certain unwise meditation procedures can cause auric damage, but one of the most certain ways of causing such a wound is by the continued practice of drug-taking. Whatever some 'advanced' psychologists may say, the continued use of drugs *does* do great damage to the aura, and opens it to all manner of invading influences.

Psychedelic Drugs

The occasional 'trip' under careful medical supervision may not have this effect, but I am in entire agreement with one of the most experienced writers in this field, and one can speak from his own personal knowledge. Dr I.F. Regardie, writing of the effect of such practices, says '... the outright psychotic person ... should be sternly counselled never, under any circumstances, to touch the psychedelic drugs.' Here he is speaking of the psychological states, and, of course, it is realized by most people who have studied this matter that few people are free from some trace of the neurotic or psychotic in their mental make-up.

More fully does this ruling apply when we are considering the etheric aura, for therein are many dim shapes which foreshadow coming trouble and conflict in both the mind and the body, for all disorders of the mind, emotions and physical body show their traces in this aura before ever they are made manifest in psychological or physical illness.

To open the surface of the aura to the play of all kinds of forces is equivalent to peeling off the protecting skin from one's body, and the dangers are as great in the one case as they would be in the other. Obviously, no one in his senses would deprive himself of his bodily skin, but because the process is not so painful, there are many who perform the psychic equivalent of this process by practices of various kinds.

Some theosophical writers would prohibit tobacco and alcohol and it is true that the social use of alcoholic beverages has blinded many to the grim fact that *addiction* to alcohol is in itself a disease, with distressing consequences. However, the school to which I subscribe does not lay down arbitrary rulings on these points, contenting itself by pointing out that if you want the best results, then you must provide the best conditions!

The etheric web not only restricts the amount of energy which may be poured out from the centres, but it also acts as a barrier to outer influences which may seek to penetrate into the etheric body, and as long as it is kept intact, then the possibilities of what I term 'psychic infection' are lessened.

Re-charging the Etheric 'Batteries'
The energies of the various centres may be projected from the aura, and such projections of power are often to be seen as either misty, cloud-like emanations or clear-cut rays or beams of light. Much depends upon the intensity of the will or desire which lies behind such a projection of energy.

Where the intensity is great, it would seem that much concentrated power may be given out in a short time, and such expenditure of energy leaves the person depleted in vitality. Under these conditions he may tend to become so negative that a kind of 'suction' is established, and he tends to draw energy from those around him or, for the matter of that, from *any* convenient source of such power. Here I may mention one method by which such a temporarily devitalized person may rapidly recharge the etheric 'batteries'.

Vitality is by no means confined to the animal and human kingdoms, of course, but most people do not realize that the members of the vegetable kingdom not only draw in etheric energy, but are also surrounded by a simple aura of such energy which is surplus to their requirements. The quality of these auras varies considerably, but there are some which blend very well with the specialized human etheric energies, and it is possible for anyone who is depleted of vitality to rapidly recharge by a simple technique.

Suitable Trees

The best trees to choose for this purpose are the pine and fir trees, oak, beech and apple being good second choices. In the grounds of the cottage in which I am writing this, we have a huge oak, several hundred years old, and the aura which it emanates is very helpful indeed. The elm is a tree to avoid as far as its auric atmosphere is concerned, for quite apart from its nasty habit of dropping a dead branch without any warning, it does seem to be in some way inimical to human beings.

However, we will imagine that you have found a suitable pine tree for your re-charging activities. You now seat yourself on the ground with your back placed firmly against the trunk of the tree. Since the ground is liable to be damp, a good waterproof cushion is indicated, and it does not matter one little bit whether it is made of rubber, plastic foam or any other material, as long as it keeps you clear of the damp ground.

There has been a good deal of nonsense written and spoken about insulation. Many people subscribe to the superstition that anything made of rubber or plastic will 'insulate' you from the etheric forces. This is just not so, as has so often been demonstrated. Water diviners who believed that rubber neutralized their powers, found that this was indeed the case, but other water diviners who did not believe in this insulating power of rubber were able to divine whilst wearing rubber soled shoes or Wellingtons.

The superstition arose, I think, because rubber *is* an insulator as far as electrical currents are concerned, and so led to the idea that the vital currents are electrical in their nature. They are, of course, but in quite a different way, and normal rubber insulation does not cut them off or interfere with their activity in any way, *unless the person concerned thinks that it will have this effect.*

The Tree Aura
Now, having seated yourself quite comfortably with your back firmly pressed against the tree trunk, you now adopt a certain attitude of mind, or rather of mind *and feeling.* For in this realm the feelings are important, you don't 'think' yourself into the tree aura, you 'feel' yourself into it, which I still find listed in Roget, i.e., 'cuddle', which had the general idea of holding in one's embrace someone with

whom one was on terms of endearment. Maybe there is a modern equivalent, though I must confess I have not heard of it.

Anyway, it is this affectionate feeling towards the simple intelligence which one might figuratively term the 'spirit of the tree' which is required. It is a feeling, not a sharply defined mental picture which is required, but a good auxiliary to this 'feeling' approach is to visualize as clearly as one can whatever symbolic form which we feel may best represent, to us, the essential nature of the tree. If, by any chance you have developed the etheric sight, then it may well be that you do actually get a glimpse of the living intelligence of which the tree is the outward and visible manifestation.

Now, without strain, but utterly relaxed in this affectionate approach to the living being which is the real tree, you simply rest, and allow the energies which are being given off by it to pass into yourself. Fifteen minutes or even less of this can effectively recharge the vitality batteries in you.

On many occasions I have used this method of renewing energy, and I know from that personal experience that it really does work. Many others have also used the method, and received benefit from it. However, the key to the whole operation is the 'feeling' rather than the 'thinking' approach to it. It even works with some who totally disbelieve in the possibility of such a vitality-transfer, people who put it all down to mere auto-suggestion. You are free to adopt this explanation if it pleases you, but I can assure you that there is more than 'mere' auto-suggestion involved in the practice.

Emanations from the Mineral Kingdom
It is also possible to become *en rapport* with the emanations which are continually being radiated from the mineral kingdom, the rocks and earth around us and upon which we live and move, though the artificial concrete jungle of our large towns often prevents us receiving these emanations except in a diluted form.

At the same time, it is in the basic etheric of the planet that we make contact, through the centre below the feet, with the great sources of vital energy, just as in the centre which is above the head we make contact with the positive forces which are the driving energies of the universe on its higher levels.

The Vital Flow
We may think of these two centres as being the two terminals which connect us to the bi-polar universe of force and form. These two centres may therefore be regarded as the two terminals of a circuit carrying an alternating current of electricity. You will see that the full flow will be hindered if *either* terminal is not properly connected to the universal supply.

I have said that this vital flow is an alternating one, going first in one direction and then in another, and anyone who does any practical occult or psychic work has to reckon with the direction of this flow at any particular time. In the east, this has been carefully worked out, but in the west there is not much detailed knowledge available except in some of the more hidden occult groups.

Modern psychology, and more particularly what

is now called 'depth psychology' has a good deal to tell us concerning this vital flow and the ways in which it may be checked and interfered with on the one hand, and increased and helped on the other.

Manifestation of Universal Energy

According to the direction of the flow of this primary or central current of the aura, will be the nature and manifestation of the universal energy. If it is flowing from the earth centre upwards, it will tend to intensify the bodily vitality and all the normal functions of the body will be strengthened. If, on the other hand, it is flowing from the head centre, then the mental aspects will predominate. But at all times, the aura will be charged with a mixed 'magnetism', and the ultimate deciding factor in how that power manifests will lie in the hands of the waking consciousness.

Though the inner forces may be stimulating aspects of our nature which we find it inconvenient or wrong to express in their basic form at the time, it is the waking consciousness which has the responsibility as to how those forces do actually show themselves in daily life.

It is here in the non-dimensional consciousness of the present that our real development always takes place. For the past is gone, the future has not yet emerged, and only the razor-edged present is ours to work with. Even as we think and speak and act, that which was present becomes the past, and the future becomes the present. Perhaps there is a profound psychological truth contained in the biblical words: '*Now* is the acceptable time; now is the day of salvation'.

The Secondary Circuit

This brings me to another point. The action of this central circuit of force builds up a secondary 'field of force' in what we have here considered as the etheric aura, and this aura has certain phases through which it has to pass.

This secondary circuit is sensitive to any outside influences which may affect it, especially before it is properly developed and when it is in a condition which, to go back to our analogy of the 'skin', is similar to the condition of a physical body deprived of its protecting skin.

Thus, this extreme sensitivity is entirely out of the control of the person concerned, and his reactions to those outside influences are correspondingly intense and irrational.

'Open' Psychics

As the general development of the individual consciousness continues, the etheric web or skin becomes more properly organized and begins to shut off the aura from many of the influences which once affected it so strongly. But where this does not happen the individual remains open to all the various outside influences which may play upon him.

This is one of the dangers which threaten those who are sometimes called 'negative psychics'. The term has been unfairly used by *some* occultists to include all those psychics of a different way of thinking to their own, but I am using it here for what has often been described as the 'open psychic'. These open psychics are the curse of any movement in which they happen to be, for with their inability to shut off unwanted influences they are like human Aeolian harps, upon which every passing wind makes sound, usually discordant.

Just as they are receptive to all influences which strike upon their aura, so are they open to every predatory influence which may desire to draw from them what vital energies they may have to give, though as a general rule, because of this leaking aura, the amount of vitality they are capable of losing in this way is small, since there is never a large supply in store.

With true development, however, the aura becomes insulated against such involuntary reactions, and the etheric centres begin to be capable of being used as perceptive organs under voluntary control.

Interesting Research

A wide field of interesting research lies before the clairvoyant who elects to work along these lines, and it is my own considered opinion that this research may well be of great use not only in what we may call the psychic field, but in the fields of medicine and electronic physics as well.

Some interesting experiments have already been made into the nature of electric currents, using the developed etheric clairvoyance of one member of a research group, but owing to the mental reactions of orthodox workers in this field, the work of this particular group has been suspended, for the time being at least. However, it may well be that sometime in the future the intellectual climate may so change that this type of research will be again carried out.

The etheric aura is not only a 'surround' or atmosphere which is the basis of the physical body. It not only receives influences but it also sends them out. The influences which are sent out from the etheric aura are of various kinds, and are capable of considerable variations in both strength and quality.

Normally, the healthy person, and by 'healthy' I also mean psychically and mentally, is constantly radiating a steady flow of etheric energies during his waking state, and this personally coloured force constitutes what we may call the personal magnetism of the man.

There is also a steady flow of vital energy from the healthy person, for he draws into himself more than sufficient of the vitalizing forces of nature, and the excess which is left after his physical body has used all it requires is radiated out in a steady stream.

Etheric Healing
Many 'healers' work with this vital energy and are able to 're-charge' those who may, for one reason or another, be depleted. There are, of course, grades of vital energy, and for this reason various healers appear to work in different ways.

There is one important thing to remember about the use of excess vital energies for the purpose of healing. When Dr Mesmer, who popularized this form of healing in France during the latter part of the eighteenth century, put forward his theories as to the energy which he claimed to be able to direct to his patients, he spoke of it as a universal 'fluid' which pervades the universe. This energy, he claimed, could be drawn upon for healing the physical body.

It was found in actual healing practice that if the 'magnetizer' or healer believed this idea of the universal fluid to be true, and held this belief firmly in his mind, he did not tend to become depleted of energy when treating many patients one after the other. On the other hand, if he regarded the powers as being his own personal power, he quickly became depleted if he treated more than a certain limited number of patients at the one session. Even when the belief in the universal fluid *was* firmly held, too long a session would produce temporary depletion, and the healer had to rest awhile.

Biblical Healing

This recalls the words attributed to Jesus when he healed the woman with the issue of blood. She touched Him in the midst of the crowd which was pressing around Him, and the disciples were quite right, of course, when He said, 'Who touched me?' to reply, 'Thou seest the crowd, and sayest thou "who touched me"?'

I have seen a similar scene in the east when a wandering *sannyasi* or holy man came into a small village. The entire population clustered around him, trying to touch him. (Incidentally, in quite another context, similar scenes can be seen, not in the far-off east, but in any town in Britain today when some idol of the pop world visits the place!)

The Bible story goes on to say that Jesus perceived that 'virtue' had gone forth from Him. This word 'virtue' was used by the King James' translators of the Authorized Version of the Bible to stand for a Greek word which is the root from which such modern words as dynamo, dynamic, and dynamite were formed. It implies a *strong, active energy* not what is usually thought of when we employ the term 'virtue'. The usual meaning attributed to the word is moral or ethical purity, more especially sexual purity.

The Power of Purity

This meaning really proceeds from the original meaning of the word, for it was widely held in ancient days that purity of life, and especially purity of sexual life, conferred a power upon a person. It was even held that a virgin girl would not be attacked by a wild beast because of her virginity! This idea also led to the insistence, in medieval magic upon the 'scryer' or seer in the magical experiments being either a boy or girl below the age of puberty.

Actually, for reasons of 'magnetic' or etheric purity there is something in this latter idea. Also, men and women of pre-eminent moral and spiritual virtue have been known to pass unharmed through the haunts of vicious and predatory wild beasts, though they were closely watched and inspected by those beasts.

The co-founder of the Theosophical Society, Col. Henry Steel Olcott, did a great deal of magnetic healing during his stay in India, and, in fact, so badly depleted himself that, upon the advice of an occult expert in such matters, he stopped this healing work, and spent some time in recuperating his energies. The chief way in which he did this was, again upon the advice of his occult friend, to sit with his back against the trunk of a pine tree, and to allow the vital energies of the tree to re-charge him.

Depletion of Personal Energies

Valentine Greatrakes in Ireland in the eighteenth century used this magnetic healing technique by what is usually known as the 'laying on of hands', and was, in fact allocated a small pension from the British Government for his work. Father John of Kronstadt, a priest of the Orthodox Church, was not so fortunate, he so depleted himself that he ultimately died as a result of his healing work.

There is a point to be noted here. Both Greatrakes and Father John regarded the power which they used as being something which was not theirs, but for which they were a channel. Why then were they so depleted? The answer is that although there may be an inexhaustible supply, unless the channels through which that power is drawn into the human personality of the healer are sufficiently clear and open enough to allow all the power needed to flow in, there will be a gradual depletion of the healer's personal energies, and the only solution, at least for the short term outlook, is to stop doing healing work until the stock of energy has been renewed.

Magnetic Healing

Magnetic healing is usually done by what is known as 'passes' made with the hands over the body of the patient, or by the 'laying-on-of-hands' or by the use of 'healing oils'. Here we come to an interesting point in the study of these etheric energies. The etheric aura is not only a receiver of forces, but also

THE CIRCUIT OF FORCE 53

a transmitter, and the energies which flow through it may be directed to other things, quite apart from human bodies.

Animals may benefit from the forces directed upon them through the etheric aura, and so also may the members of the vegetable kingdom. I have referred to the energy which Col. Olcott drew from the pine tree, but this is not a one-way traffic. Just as we can draw etheric energy from the plants and trees, so can they draw from us when they, in their turn, need such help.

There have been many experiments made in this power of some human beings to affect for good or bad the lives of members of the vegetable kingdom, and it may well be that those who possess the traditional 'green-fingers' are people with the power to transmit these energies to an ailing plant.

That these people do not consciously realize their possession of this power does not matter in the least; in fact it may often help, since their conscious mind is for the moment out of the way, and the subconscious has a chance to bring the etheric mechanism into action.

But not only can the etheric energies be transmitted to human beings, animals and plants. They can also be poured into and 'charge' inanimate objects such as stones, jewels, oils, and so on. These objects will then act as a kind of magnetic battery, pouring their charge of energy out as required.

Where this 'charging' or 'magnetizing' is done by someone who understands the principles involved, then the object so charged becomes not merely a battery which will discharge itself until its charge is exhausted, but will also be linked up with the universal energies, and so remain charged and potent for healing, or for any other purpose for which it was originally intended.

In the Roman Church the *Oleum Infirmorum*, the oil for the sick, is blessed by the bishop in his cathedral church on Maundy Thursday for use during the following year. However, healing oil may be prepared by anyone who understands the principle of magnetization.

A Cure with Oils

That the use of the healing oils may be effective was once demonstrated to me. It was in January of 1919, and I was at that time a patient in the Military Hospital in Glasgow, having been invalided from France in 1918. During my convalescence, I was invited to a healing demonstration which was being done by a small group of 'metaphysical' healers. Their technique was to surround the patient with thoughts of healing, and to call down, from higher levels, the universal healing force.

As it was known that I was a clairvoyant, they asked me to report on what I might see during the healing. This I did, and I was able to tell them that although the patient appeared to be surrounded by a deep blue cloud of energy, none of it was entering her body; it simply lay there like a pool of blue light enveloping her. She herself, on being questioned, said that she felt no different, and certainly no better.

It so happened that another occultist who was

also present, had some of the healing oils in his pocket, and it was suggested that he should use them on the patient. So un-stoppering the small silver tube in which the healing oil was kept, he moistened his thumb with oil and just traced the sign of the Cross on the forehead of the patient.

A Vortex

At once things began to happen. To my sight it was as though a vortex was set up over the forehead of the subject, and the deep blue light seemed to pour down this in almost exactly the same way as the water in the bath or sink disappears when the plug is removed. Within a short time, all the energy had been absorbed into the patient's body. Not only did she say she felt much better, it was clearly evident that she was brighter and more alert, and appeared to be much improved.

It was explained that the magnetized oil had acted as a bridge between the finer energies which had been drawn down upon the patient and her own etheric body and aura. It was then possible for that energy to be drawn into the etheric aura and so made of some use.

A similar technique is used by some healers who 'magnetize' handkerchieves or linen pads and send them to their patients, and in this connection one thinks of the objects which were taken to the sick because the shadow of one of the Apostles had fallen on them. If we read 'aura' for 'shadow', we may see some significance in the Bible story.

The field of force which we call the etheric aura is the field in which many as yet unsuspected energies play. All the facts about the aura have yet to be discovered, and there are many fascinating lines of research for those so interested.

Etheric Interaction

The interactions between the etheric auras of people is another most interesting phenomenon. The 'spell-binder' who can charm the birds down out of the trees, as the saying goes, has this ability because of a certain development in his etheric aura, and his intellectual or oratorical attainments have nothing to do with this power.

There are others who act as destructive catalysts, and who, in any group, irrespective of what they may say or not say, will cause disruption and dissension. In the same way there are those who, because they are catalysts of the opposite order, will enable the members of a group to work together in an almost incredible fashion.

Again, there are some who have the peculiar power to bring into action the latent abilities of others. This is noticeable in cases where a teacher who has a strong sense of vocation, apart from the purely material and professional aspect of his work, appears to be able to make such an intimate contact with the minds of his pupils as to evoke from them their own innate powers in a way that the ordinary teacher very often signally fails to do.

'Developing Circles'

A curious variant of this power is that possessed by some who, by their presence alone, stimulate into activity the psychic abilities of those around them, though they themselves often display no such powers. Such people are useful members of what are known as 'developing circles'. It would seem that some part of their etheric aura has the property of inducing its own rate of vibration in the auras of others.

Here we may also speculate as to whether the universal custom of the laying-on-of-hands for the transmission of priestly and other offices may not have a basis in this property of the etheric. This would, of course, be strongly denied by those who, in this egalitarian age, vociferously insist that all men are equal and that no one has any power or ability which others have not got also. One might reply to this claim by suggesting that the ideal society would be one where each member brought his own particular and, perhaps, unique gift into the common pool for the benefit of all.

CHAPTER FOUR

THE EMOTIONAL-MENTAL AURA

It is the custom of many writers on occult subjects to make a clear-cut and definite division between the emotional and mental aspects of man's nature, and when considering the structure of the human entity to refer to the 'emotional or astral body' and the 'mental body' as two entirely separate parts of his being. This is, of course, quite correct if you are conducting what we might describe as a post-mortem on the complete man; that is, if you are studying him as an anatomist studies the human body.

To the anatomist, there are certain well-defined systems of organs, nerves, etc., and these he sees, first of all as separate systems, such as the alimentary system, the vascular system, and so on, even though he always keeps at the back of his mind the over-riding fact that all these systems in the living man are working together in a very wonderful way, and their individual activities are joined together for the common life of the individual.

Equally, of course, it is permissible to separate the emotional and mental aspects of man, and also the 'vehicles' or 'bodies' through which those aspects work, but when we come to consider the living individual, we find that in actual practice we cannot separate these two ways in which man expresses himself on the physical plane.

The Kama-Manasic Principle

This has been recognized in both the eastern and western occult traditions. In the east, the two activities of emotion and thought are grouped together under the term *Kama-Manas*, *Kama* meaning 'desire' and *Manas* referring to 'mind'. Above this double aspect they also refer to the plane or level of *pure* thought by the term 'The *Manasic* Plane'.

In the western tradition the same idea is found in the Qabalistic concept of what is termed the *Ruach* or 'reasonable soul'. They too say that above this realm there exists another region wherein that aspect of man which the Qabalists name the *Neschamah* or Higher Soul has its dwelling.

Although I follow the western esoteric tradition, I am going to briefly attempt to separate these two elements of emotion and thought which go to make up the *Ruach* or *Kama-manasic* principle in man. I propose to deal with the emotional or 'astral' aspect as being one in which 'force' is predominant.

Fundamental Duality

There is a certain fundamental duality throughout the whole of the kingdoms of nature – a division into realms of 'force' and realms of 'form'. Each level is made up of these two aspects, but the proportions vary with the different levels of manifestation.

Thus, the physical earth is a plane of 'form', but it is actually the appearance which is the result of interlocked forces. Its chief characteristic is that of *inertia*. It is a level of stability, and physical matter will not of itself change position unless acted upon by some outer force. The etheric levels of the

physical are the 'force' aspect, and matter as we see
it is the 'form' aspect of this physical level.

On the emotional or 'astral' level, the positions
are reversed. The substance of the astral light is
characterized by extreme mobility; it is 'fluidique'
and has the Protean ability to take a thousand
evanescent shapes as different influences affect it. In
itself it can best be thought of as a realm of living
light; light which can in an instant be built up into
a temporary form.

Symbols

There are two main building or form-producing
causes at work in the astral realms. One is the
influence which is always at work moulding the
tenuous astral substance in obedience to its own
basic laws. These forms which are, so to speak,
native to the astral light, cannot be perceived by the
average human clairvoyant, for they are so far from
all human experience that there is nothing in the
clairvoyant's mind by which such forms can be
comprehended.

The only way in which these native forms can be
brought into the waking consciousness is by the
deliberate use of *symbols*, and it is for this reason
that many seers have found it necessary to resort to
the use of symbolism to transmit even a small part
of the astral perception through to the conscious
mind.

But such use of symbols demands considerable
training in their use and understanding so those
who have not undergone a definite training along
those lines do not, as a general rule perceive the
native forms in the astral light, except where certain

well-established symbols have been constructed by generations of men. Then, under earthly veils, these things are perceived.

Form from Mental Activity

The other form building process on the levels of the astral light is that of *thought*, both conscious and subconscious. The mental levels are 'form' levels, as opposed to the 'force' levels of the astral light, and it is the form produced by mental activity which is thrown into the astral realms and which immediately becomes charged with the force of that level. So in the astral light, there are to be found multitudinous images built up by the action of thought from the plastic fluidic substance of that level.

Some of these forms and images are as transient as the ripple produced by the passing breeze playing upon the still surface of a lake, but others are far more lasting, and provide the semi-permanent scenery of the astral world. Of such are the 'heavens' and 'hells' and 'grey worlds' so commonly described in spiritualist literature, and to those who live in them they do constitute a scenery and background which reflects, to a greater or lesser degree the scenery and conditions of the earth itself.

The thoughts which produce these 'mansions', these temporary resting-places of the human spirit in the astral world, are the results of conscious and subconscious thinking on the part of humanity both incarnate and discarnate, as well as the mental activity of other non-human life which shares this level with man and which closely influences him, though he may not be aware of it.

I cannot go into greater detail concerning these astral levels in the limited scope of this book, but I have mentioned this power of the mind to build forms, and for those forms composed of astral substance to last for a longer or shorter time because the astro-mental aura which is present around each one of us is a field in which these same laws are at work.

Our thinking builds forms in our astro-mental aura, even as the collective thinking of the whole of humanity builds up the forms in the astral light, or, to give it its modern name, the collective unconscious.

Second Aura

So, to the clairvoyant eye, the aura appears as a luminous coloured atmosphere surrounding everyone. The extent of this second aura will vary according to the emotional and mental development of the person observed, as will also its colouring. This colouring will range from dark and muddy looking shades of brown and grey, through lurid reds and dirty looking blues, to the finer shades of these colours and to fine luminous yellow, blue and violet shades. There may also appear gleams of pure golden light, but these are usually rare.

In this shining atmosphere around each person may also be noticed 'forms' of various kinds, and it is here that mistakes may often arise when a description of the aura is being given. There are often human figures to be seen in the aura, but these need not be anything to do with the actual life, being merely thought-forms which have been built up by casual contacts with people who, for one reason or another, have left a strong imprint on the mind of the person whose aura is being observed.

Subconscious Memories

There are other finer and more subtle forms which are often only outcropping memories from the subconscious, and, indeed, it sometimes happens that something is described by the seer, and is immediately recognized by the person concerned. Very often he will say, 'It couldn't be telepathy, for I wasn't thinking about that thing at all'.

However, this is what it could probably be in truth, since these thought-forms can act as the end of a long line of associated memories which are evoked, as it were, from the depths of the subconsciousness. Of course, this does not cover all such forms, but it certainly seems to account for a good deal of so-called 'evidence'.

Occasionally such forms seen and described by the clairvoyant turn out to be nothing more than vivid images built up in the mind of a person through reading a book which portrays such characters. Thus one lady was told by a clairvoyant, 'I see a strange figure with you. Have you anything to do with the sea? For I see the figure of a man who would be a seaman of some kind, and who possibly fought in some sea battle, for I see he has only one leg. I see around him what seems to be tropical vegetation and I get a strong feeling of violence and bloodshed.'

The person to whom this description was given smiled and said 'Yes, I recognize the figure – you

see I have just been reading Robert Louis
Stevenson's book *Treasure Island*!'

It is difficult for even the experienced seer to
always detect the difference between these thought-
forms and other forms which may come into the
aura from other sources. Only practice over a long
period will enable him to do this, and even then he
may often be mistaken.

The second part of the emotional-mental aura is
the luminous appearance which spreads around the
person. In some it may only extend about a couple
of feet, but with others its range is far more
extensive. It remains now to deal with this luminous
atmosphere from a consideration of the colours
which are to be found in it.

Spirit and Matter not Opposed

Here I must say that often the mistake is made of
equating the finer pastel shades of colour with the
'spiritual' nature, whilst the more vivid and denser
shades are held to be indications of the 'earthly'
side of the self. Now this is a mistaken view. It is
true to a certain point, but it often gives a totally
false idea of the character of the person.

First of all, such a view accepts the idea of
'material' and 'spiritual' as being two sharply
divided opposites like the east and west in Kipling's
poem, 'Never the twain shall meet'. This was the
error of the Gnostics, or *some* of them, in the early
Christian Church, and in one form or another it has
persisted through the centuries.

The truer view, in the opinion of many of us, is
that both 'spirit' and 'matter' are the expressions of
a supreme reality; they are, as it were, the two poles

of the cosmic battery, and the web of the universe is spun between them. In that 'field of energies' all life and consciousness lives and moves and has its being. There are two institutions wherein this is symbolized by the two Pillars of Solomon's Temple; between these lies the tessellated pavement of black and white squares, and our human pilgrimage means that we are never wholly treading upon a black square or entirely upon a white one.

A Mixed Bag

This is reflected in our individual private universe, and reveals itself in the aura. It is an over-simplification to divide humanity into 'goodies' and 'baddies', in the tradition of the Wild West films. We are a mixed bag, and there are both good and evil aspects in each one of us. There used to be a doggerel rhyme which stated, 'There's so much good in the worst of us, and so much bad in the best of us,' and this is true.

There are aspects of our nature which are of the higher part, and there are other aspects which are of the lower side of ourselves, and there is a large part of our emotional-mental make-up which is the reflection of a mixture of both of these aspects, and according to the general activity of these factors so we build up what we may term the permanent background of the aura.

It is this general colouring which usually shows us as we are, and this is fairly stable, changing slowly or otherwise as we progress through life.

However, there are times when the more elemental parts of our nature suddenly emerge into activity, and their activity is shown by the fiery and turbid shades of colour which show themselves in the aura. In the same way, there are times when the ethical and spiritual aspects of ourselves also come into activity, and such activity is shown by the finer shades of colour.

But both of these conditions may only be, most probably *will* be, of short duration, and their appearance does not give a clue as to the real character of the person in whose aura they are seen.

Significance of Pastel Shades

Often an aura showing all the colours in fine pastel shades may well indicate a personality without any positive will or emotional 'drive', and such people, although regarded by their friends as most 'spiritual', are only to be so thought of in a negative way. I think it is Milton who somewhere says, 'I would not praise a cloistered virtue which has never been subjected to temptation.'

In the same way, the aura very often indicates that, far from its possessor being 'highly evolved' he is, in fact, quite 'unevolved' in some important ways, and it may also indicate the near total repression of part of the nature.

Because of this, it is difficult to correctly assess the true level of character of anyone by simply reading his aura, unless one has built up by practice the ability to watch the 'permanent aura' when the nature is being subjected to stress. It is under these conditions that the true character of a person can be discerned.

Suppression is not Control

I have told the following story before in another book of mine, but it will bear repetition, as it illustrates a mistake so many make in supposing that the *suppression* of all physical signs of any particular emotion indicates that one has gained *control* over it.

In a certain occult training college (for such establishments really do exist) the principal had a technique of his own. Each of the students had a small garden for which they were directly responsible. All these gardens were visible from the dining room and it sometimes happened that whilst at dinner, a student would look through the window and see his or her little garden being ruined by the activities of one of several animals which were kept at the place.

The students were supposed to look at this wanton destruction without any display of emotion, even though it meant that many hours of work had passed in vain. (The presence of the animal in the garden concerned had been carefully engineered by the principal himself.)

The one who told me of this, who was herself one of these students, said that she found herself perfectly able to watch her gardening efforts being brought to naught because, as she put it, she had been blessed with a good 'poker face'! Under her calm and placid appearance, however, she was seething with indignation and busy working out various punishments which might fit the crime.

It is far better to release such emotions than to repress them violently into the depths of the mind, and, of course, it is better still to learn to control the *inner* reactions rather than the physical expressions thereof. Such repressions result in a churning up of the mind which is reflected in the aura.

Projection of Thought-forms

Incidentally, in the emotional-mental aura there are to be found many forms which have been built up in the mind, but most of these are vague and indistinct. The emotional-mental aura, like the etheric aura, has an outer limit which seems to act as a kind of protective 'skin', though the radiations of the aura pass through it for considerable distances.

It is through these radiations that what we call 'telepathy' takes place, but most of the thought-forms built up in the aura never have the energy needed to protect them beyond the outer limit of their creator's aura. Like sparks from the blacksmith's anvil, when the white-hot iron is struck by the hammer, such thought-sparks fly upwards, but are almost immediately quenched and never go beyond the brief area around them.

Two things are necessary for the successful projection of such thought-forms beyond the aura, and these two things are clearness of form and strength of 'charge'.

The successful building up of forms in the mind is something which cannot usually be acquired in a short time; it takes a period of steady training, unless the one who is building the forms has some innate ability in this direction. This does sometimes happen, and then, one of the conditions being fulfilled, it remains to see how the form can be charged with the energy which will enable it to be projected to a distance.

This is done by a process of 'brooding over' the thought, and by 'brooding over' I mean a steady *emotional* concentration upon it. It is for this reason that so many experiments in thought-transference fail.

The form of the thought may have been visualized and built up clearly, but since no emotional force is connected with it, there is no power to project it upon its way. Also, over a long continued run of tests using the Zener Cards, the interest and therefore the enthusiasm (which is really a 'feeling') slacken, and the psychic faculty ceases to work. This is not always the case, for there is some evidence to suggest that, *sometimes*, the receiver's mind reaches out towards the mind of the sender, and reads therein the picture or symbol which he is wishing to transmit.

Dissociated Complexes

The thought-forms which accumulate within the aura because of suppression and inhibition have a strong influence upon the character of the individual, and even more so are those emotionally charged groups of thoughts which are known to the psychologists as 'dissociated complexes'. These thoughts have been thrust out from the normal circulation of the mind, and have become semi-independent.

Because of the strong emotional 'charge' within dissociated complexes, they come into conflict with the normal processes of the mind, and the resulting battle means that most of the available energy of the personality is locked up and cannot be used. So arise the various troubles which are the symptoms of this underlying fight and it is vitally important in every way that some contact with this semi-independent complex which is throttling the inflow of energy should be gained.

Modern psychologists have a useful method of doing this – the so-called 'word association test'. Certain words are said to the patient, and he is asked to give the first word which comes into his mind as soon as he has heard the test word. The time before he is able to produce such a word, which arises from the depths within him, varies widely.

With some of the association words the patient will produce his own reaction-word almost immediately, but with others there is often a complete inability to produce any reaction, or a reaction word will only come up in his mind after quite a long time. The actual reaction times are usually taken by means of a stop-watch.

Self-Protective Device

This method has proved helpful, though it has also been found that a certain self-protective device in the subconsciousness has produced a 'substitute' reaction word, in order to stop any further probing. Sometimes, such substitute words may be as revealing as those for which they stand, but on the other hand, they may be wildly misleading.

The reaction word is used as the beginning of a chain of what is known as 'free association', as the patient is asked to let his mind go free and allow the reaction word to start any trains of thought it will. By the use of several of the test words, several such trains of 'free association' may be started, and they will often be found to be converging towards some central idea.

Somewhere in this region lies the contact with the semi-independent thought-complex and if it is successfully contacted, then the repressed thoughts and memories surge up into consciousness, together with the powerful charge of energy which they have held, and, after a period of readjustment, the patient's mind is restored to normal working.

Gentle Disclosure

However, if by the use of psychic vision the dissociated complex can be seen in the emotional-mental aura of the patient, it is then possible to *gently* disclose it to the patient, thus avoiding the distressing uprush of emotional energy which so often happens when the complex is contacted. The 're-education' as it is called, whereby the *cause* of the dissociation can be removed from the personality, can then proceed much more rapidly than otherwise.

An additional advantage possessed by this method is that where the patient's subconscious mind has shown itself capable of fabricating imaginary 'memories' and situations of the past, it is possible to get behind the defences, as it were, and see direct into the creative area of the mind and so cease to be deceived by the phantasies which the sick mind may build up.

Some years ago I knew a psychic who discovered that she possessed this ability to see the thought-forms within the aura of patients undergoing psycho-analytical treatment, and as she said, she found herself able to proceed directly to the re-education of the mind without going through the lengthy and often distressing procedure involved in the usual word tests.

As the lady was at that time a worker with a quite orthodox (in the medical sense) clinic in London, and was also one of the first *lay* psycho-analysts in this country, her testimony may be thought to be of value.

Meanings of the Colours

I have refrained from giving any 'meanings' to the colours which may be seen in the aura. There are several books which give the conventional meanings, but in my own experience I have found that almost every person who develops psychic vision tends to have his own individual meaning which he attaches to the colours he sees, and *for him* these meanings are correct. Another psychic may well have a different set of meanings, and for him these may also be correct.

The trouble arises when an attempt is made to enforce a system which shall be true for all. It can be done, and in certain occult schools it *is* done, but it' takes a lot of hard work, and as long as the clairvoyant finds that *his* interpretations of the colours he sees are correct, he may well leave his brother psychic to the use of *his* system.

Purity of the Colours

One point which all clairvoyants are agreed upon is the *purity* of the colours seen, and by this I do not mean the pale pastel shades, which are usually indicative of repressed or depleted vitality.

A colour can be strong as well as clear; what is necessary is that it shall not be contaminated by any mixture from another colour. Now the images and thoughts derived from the experiences of earth are all to some extent so contaminated, although the degree may vary, and in the same way the images and thoughts which are influenced by the realms of the upper mind and spirit are usually irradiated by a starry luminosity which is quite unlike anything to be found in this material level.

So the way in which the colours are shaded by earthly hues, or illumined by the starry radiance of the realms of true mind and spirit will give to the clairvoyant some indication of the general character of the person observed, but it is only when the aura is observed during a time when its owner is under the test of trial and temptation that the *true* character can be gauged.

A Wonderful Sight

The truly spiritual aura appears as a pervading radiance which informs both the etheric and emotional-mental auras, and streams beyond them, and in one who is advanced on the spiritual path it is one of the most wonderful sights which can ever be seen by the seer. At the same time, it should be observed that any clairvoyant will as a general rule see only that to which he himself can respond, and consequently, the higher aspects of what a recent writer has called 'The Robe of Many Colours' are far beyond the reach of the average clairvoyant.

There are many fascinating things concerning this astromental aura and the forms and forces to be seen therein which I have been unable to touch upon within the compass of this book, but I hope that sufficient has been given to interest and help those who may now or in the future essay to work along these lines of study and research.

CHAPTER FIVE

DEVELOPING AURIC SIGHT

There are several ways in which auric sight may be developed. One of these, as I have indicated in another book, is to use what are known as the 'Kilner Screens', named after their inventor, Dr Kilner. These consist of glass cells containing a solution of certain dyes, usually 'dycyanine' and 'pinacol', both coal tar derivatives. By looking through the coloured liquid in the cells at a source of light for a period, the mechanism of the eyes is slightly changed, and it begins to respond to the etheric emanations given off from the body. Full details of the procedure to be adopted are given by the manufacturers of these 'auric goggles'.*

Reading the Aura by Touch
However, it may not be possible for you to obtain such goggles, and you are then forced to use one of the other methods. Curiously enough, one method of reading the aura is by *touch*! This is a method calling for great care, as it is somewhat difficult, especially in the early stages, to get a clear idea of what you are really getting. The way of using the sense of touch for auric perception is as follows.

First you enlist the services of a sympathetic

* As far as I am aware, these goggles are made solely by The Society of Metaphysicians, Archers Court, Hastings, Sussex, to whom all enquiries should be addressed.

friend. He either sits in a straight-backed chair, or else lies on a couch. Then you pass your hand slowly downwards over his body, keeping it about two or three inches away from the actual surface of the body. This is most important; *never actually touch the physical body of your subject. It is not necessary and will indeed, prevent you doing any 'sensing' of his aura.* I have italicized this last sentence because I have known this instruction to be ignored by some whose motives were somewhat mixed and had very little to do with auric research.

Now, as you slowly pass your hand downwards over the subject, focus your attention upon the tips of your fingers, and try to sense any difference in the sensations you have in them as you move your hand away for about eight or nine inches, or bring it to about a couple of inches from the body.

At first, and for a good many attempts, you may perceive nothing, but this is often because you have never had to concentrate upon your fingertips in this way, and other sensations will overpower the fine impressions which you may be receiving.

There will come a time, however, when you will perceive that 'something' which seems warm or cold or vibrant appears to be present some distance from the surface of the physical body of your subject. When you have experienced this, then you can go to work to find out just how far from the subject's body this 'something' extends, and you will then be able to experiment to see what shape the 'field of force' takes.

Rough Drawings
It is good training technique to spend some time

before the experiments in preparing a number of rough drawings of the human body, front, back and side views; these could be made on a Roneo stencil, and a number of copies run off, or they could be done with hectograph ink and transferred to a 'jelly-graph' duplicator and a number of copies made. The drawings can then be used in marking down the variations which you may find to exist in the aura.

This first aura which you will be observing is, of course, the etheric aura. Later you will wish to try to perceive the astro-mental aura which as I have said, extends a good deal farther out from the body, and you will then move your hands at a greater distance, say a foot or so from the physical body of your subject.

Silvery Replica

Now it may well happen, though not in all cases, that as you begin to perceive or 'sense' the aura, pictures will build up in your mind, and these may take the form of a silvery replica of the subject's body, and this replica will show the same variations which you are sensing in the aura. You will be seeing the aura subjectively, and this is a quite common form of development. At the same time, there are many who never 'see' anything at all, but who *do* get a clear perception of the aura, its variations and other peculiarities.

So do not be discouraged if you do not develop the subjective visual perception; the non-visual intuitive perception may be far more accurate once you have learnt to trust it. It has been described as 'seeing a black cat at midnight at the bottom of a coal-mine', and although this may sound ridiculous, I can assure you, from my own personal experience of this type of vision, that you really do 'see the black cat', and what is more, you learn more about him than you might have done if you had actually perceived him visually.

Intuitive Perception of Thought-forms

The other images which may form in your mind as visual pictures, or be perceived intuitively, are usually the thought-forms which are in the aura, and these are of two main varieties.

One group is made up of those thought-forms which are the results of the mental and emotional activity of the person himself, and the other group is composed of those forms which have been built up by other people.

There are several reasons why these latter forms should be found in the aura. Sometimes they have been projected towards the person by others who have been thinking clearly and intensely about him, and have put a good deal of emotion into the process. This gives the forms their motive power and they are 'projected' beyond their auric boundary and arrive with sufficient force to enable them to lodge in the aura of the one to whom they have been directed.

This projection may be entirely unconsciously initiated; the one who is thinking so intensely of another person may not dream that he is possibly sending out such a form. There are others, however, who have a good working knowledge of this process, and are well aware of what they are doing.

Those who have been wisely instructed do not do

this kind of psychic trespass, for the penetration of the aura of another person in this way is the 'breaking of a superficies' – the 'removing of his neighbour's landmarks', and in both the Craft and in the Bible such a proceeding is regarded as wrong, and as meriting punishment.*

Where, however, the surface of the aura is loose and not strongly built up, then it will easily take in any thought-forms which may strike upon it, and such people go around with an aura which, from the clairvoyant point of view, is decidedly septic!

Because of this poorly built auric 'skin', it is sufficient for such people to pick up, like human fly-papers, any forms which may be about, and such forms may not always be of an exalted kind. Such people also 'leak' vitality, and develop what is known as the 'orbicular wound'.

Physical and Emotional-Mental Stability

As you begin to develop your ability to perceive these things, you will also find that you become aware of the measures which should be taken if the person concerned is to be brought back to full physical and emotional-mental stability. I have included this last remark because it often assists in the successful development of auric vision if you have a definite feeling that by the use of such vision you may possibly be of help to others.

Man is what has been described as a 'gregarious animal', which simply means that it is natural for us to group together, and in the conditions which this causes, most people find that to be able to help

* See Deut: 27.17.

others in some way or other gives them an increased pleasure in living. Of course, this basic urge in man is often smothered beneath a code of selfishness and egotism, but every now and then it shows itself, often in the most unlikely people.

When this desire to help does emerge its satisfaction brings to most of us a feeling that in some way we have moved beyond ourselves, and in a mysterious fashion enlarged ourselves. Although we may deviate considerably from the idea of selfless service, yet as we develop, our general inclination will be to make use of these faculties in the service of others as well as ourselves.

Auric Sight by Direct Vision

There is yet another way in which this faculty of auric sight may be developed, and that is by direct vision. At the same time, there is a trap into which you may easily fall, which consists of staring in such a fixed way at the person that the mechanism of your eyes becomes fatigued and shifts the focus and consequently the position of the image which is falling upon the retina: the screen of the eye.

The resulting flash of colour, usually yellow or golden which appears around the person being observed is often mistaken for the aura, whereas it is simply the result of optical fatigue.

So in attempting this particular way of seeing the aura, you must not stare fixedly at the person. The best results are obtained when the one whom you are observing stands against a dark background, with a north light for preference.

As you are trying to see a fine emanation which may at first, since the etheric aura is the most easily perceived at the beginning of development, be only some two inches away from the surface of the body, it is best if the subject of your vision wears close-fitting clothes. Indeed, many people find that they get the best results when the clothing worn consists simply of vest and trousers, or swimming trunks.

Here, of course, you must use your common sense. A married man who insisted upon observing a bikini clad damsel would possibly be asking for trouble, unless she was his wife. If I seem (as some of my previous remarks would suggest) somewhat prudish in my attitude towards this question of near-nudity, it is because I have had a fairly lengthy experience of these matters over a period of fifty years, and in any case it is inadvisable to introduce unnecessary distractions in an exercise which is difficult enough by itself!

Re-focusing the Eye

The subject now standing against the dark background, the observer sits and gazes quietly and without any strain at him, at the same time *throwing the eyes slightly out of focus*. This is done by actually focusing them about six to nine inches beyond the subject. This will mean that his actual form will be only vaguely discernible, although its general outlines will be sufficiently clear.

This re-focusing of the eye is a little trick which it may take some time for you to master, but by *quietly* and repeatedly attempting it, you will eventually gain proficiency. I have emphasized 'quietly', for there must be no strain, no undue physical effort.

The faculty which you are attempting to 'develop' is already within your subconscious mind, and, indeed, the better word would be *unfoldment*, rather than *development*. Any conscious effort will simply get in the way of the emergence of the faculty.

Allowing the Faculty to Unfold

It is helpful if, before you start the session, you sit down quietly, relax as well as you are able, and then, again without any strain, quietly tell yourself, and this of course includes your subconscious self, that you are now going to allow the faculty of supernormal vision to unfold itself.

You can use whatever form of words you like, as long as they convey the idea, and are positive in their meaning. For instance, you would not tell yourself that you are going to 'try' to unfold your vision. This is not positive enough.

You are now *going to allow* the faculty to unfold. How far it does actually unfold itself in any one session is something which you will not be able to gauge, but you may rest assured that every time you so affirm your intention to allow it to take place, *some* unfoldment will actually occur.

Misty Grey Luminosity

When you have mastered the technique of refocusing the eyes, and the parallel technique of the positive intention, you may begin to look out for anything which you may perceive around the subject. Usually it will take the form of a misty grey luminosity which seems to extend around the subject's body, and it is as well if, at this stage, you check to make sure that you have not inadvertently begun to use a fixed stare.

If you find that this is not the case, and that you are really seeing this luminous haze around the subject, you can then go on to note any peculiarities which may affect the aura. For instance, it may have a pronounced bulge over one particular part of the body, or it may have sunk back almost to the surface of the body. Using the sketches of the human figure in outline you should note this down, *after* the observation is finished.

If you try to see and mark out at the same time, you will find that the activity so caused will tend to break your vision. Of course you could have a tape recorder running, and by having the various parts of your outline diagram numbered, it would be possible for you to quietly observe, 'There's a big bulge over section 7' or wherever it may be seen.

What usually happens in the first session in which you actually do see anything is that your excitement tends to arouse you from the particular mental state which you have reached, and the vision is lost for that time at least. With practice, however, you learn not to allow any unwanted emotion to blur the surface of the mental mirror which is reflecting the impressions which are coming in by way of the subconscious.

The subject should change position and stand sideways to you for a time. Or put his hand upon his hip and so allow you to look for the somewhat denser aura which will be in the space between his arms and his body.

The Fingers Experiment
Then, to give the subject a rest, you can conduct a few experiments for yourself by holding your two

hands with the fingers almost touching each other
and then slowly move them apart, using the same
dark background. You will see, if the faculty is
beginning to work, what appear to be bands of
greyish light which run from the fingers of one hand
to those of the other. Now this could again be an
optical illusion, and this you may test by lowering
one hand six or nine inches below the other. You
will then see how these rays still connect the fingers,
but are now running in a diagonal direction
between them.

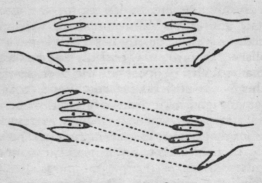

Rays between the fingers.

At a later date you can try to project the grey
light from any one selected finger, and see what
happens. Also you can see whether these rays will
flow between your hand and that of your friend, the
subject. Try the two right hands and then the two
left hands, and then the left and right hands of you
both and see what difference it makes. There are
interesting 'polarity effects' which you may notice,

and these will suggest other experiments which you
may carry out.

Auras of Plants

After you have begun to perceive the aura, and as
an interesting variant on observing the auras of
people, you may try, using the same general
technique of lighting, etc., to observe the auras of
plants and, when outside conditions permit, the
auras of trees. At a later date, you should extend
your observations to cover the radiations given off
by minerals of various kinds.

All such experiments can be of the greatest
interest, and if careful records are kept, more
especially when the faculty is becoming fairly well
established, then you may possibly discover aspects
of the aura which have not hitherto been described.
For this is a large field of research, and those who
use the power of auric vision are usually operating
in one sector only, depending upon whether they
are working with a religious group, a research
group, a magical group, or simply as solitary
students of the subject.

Although I have dealt with 'clairvoyance' and
'psychometry' in other books, it is well to realize
that these are but the separate manifestations of the
one faculty of psychic perception. The clairvoyant
and psychometric powers are but specialized
expressions of this one psychic sense, and in actual
practice you will often find that one aspect shades
off into one of the others. As a general rule this does
not matter greatly, unless you are working
exclusively along one line of work.

Patience is Essential

Finally, I would like to briefly mention the time factor. No one can tell you how long it may be before you develop the faculty, for this depends on so many considerations. A friend of mine sitting for this development, took seven years before he had *any* results whatsoever. This was an extreme case, but you must be prepared to exercise quite a lot of patience, unless you are one of those in whom the faculty is near the surface of consciousness.

Always remember, however, that *true* development should result in a well balanced character. It is far better to have five senses and sanity than to have acquired a sixth sense which causes you to be unbalanced and unreliable in your personal and social life. So it is as well, if you decide to develop this, or any other psychic faculty, to carefully consider your present personality, and try to assess your readiness for such psychic development.

Adverse Criticism

As we are usually the worst possible judges of our own personalities, it is helpful to try to get the opinions of those with whom we come into fairly close contact, and this does *not* mean that you should choose as your critics only those with whom you are on friendly terms.

A great deal can be learnt from someone who dislikes you, and who is not afraid to tell you so to your face. It could be, of course, that in some of his judgments he is wrong, as he may not be in a position to know all the things in your life which make you to be as you appear to him. Allowing for this, it may still be true that his criticism is of more value to you than perhaps the kindly evaluation of your friends! In any case, it is always a good mental and moral discipline to be strong enough to consider such adverse criticism without reacting to it in an emotional and ill-balanced way.

Remember that what you are inviting criticism upon is the unfinished temple of your personality. Any defect which you are now building into it may well imperil the whole structure when, at a later date, it is subjected to greater strain.

It is, therefore, true wisdom to consider the critic who points to defects and deficiencies, and then take a long cool look at these alleged defects and deficiencies. It may well be that some of them have been overstressed, but it may also be true that in some measure they are to be regarded as things which *are* to be seen in your personality, and they should be attended to before you go on to attempt the building of a new aspect of your personal temple.

The Safeguard of Humility

There is yet another way in which you may err in these matters. When you have at last developed the faculty, it is easy to form an exaggerated idea of your own importance, and to feel that you ought to be regarded as 'Sir Oracle'. This is a common temptation, and one which is almost certain to be ministered to by unwise friends who will attempt to put you upon a pedestal from which you may deliver the oracles of the gods.

I have mentioned this in previous books because it is one of the most common troubles in the whole of the field of psychic development, and it can lead to untold trouble.

Sooner or later, due to the natural fluctuations of the psychic perceptions, the time comes when you are no longer able to deliver the goods, and if you are honest and admit that for the time you are not able to fulfil the demands which are made on you, you will probably be somewhat surprised to find with what indecent rapidity you are removed from the seat of the oracle, and your followers go hunting for another who, in his turn, they may elevate to that position!

It is best, then, at all times, to be modest in your claims. Those who are really interested and sincere will not hold it against you that at certain times you cannot give what is wanted, nor will they be inclined to cavil because you do not make any high sounding claims for yourself and your gift.

Commercial Use of Psychic Faculties

It is for this reason, amongst others, that the occult schools usually impress upon their pupils that they must not use the psychic faculties which they develop for monetary end. The commercial use of the psychic faculties brings many temptations, chief among which is the tendency to indulge in fraud when the faculty is having one of its off-days. There are those who claim that the 'positive' seer never has off-days, and tend to regard in a supercilious fashion those who admit to such lapses.

However, in many years of practical experience in this field, I have come to the conclusion that the distinction cannot be upheld. The 'positive' seer may be less prone to such things than his 'negative' brother, but I have no doubt that at times, even for him, 'the heavens are as brass' and he gets little or nothing through his psychic faculties.

If you are free from the necessity of having to demonstrate the psychic faculty for payment, then you are free from many of the troubles which may otherwise come upon you. What is more, you will be able to express your own opinion in these fields without the fear of annoying those upon whose good-will your finances depend.

Religious Organizations

The development of the psychic faculties has hitherto been mainly under the aegis of religious organizations, and they have been pressed into service to prove this or that tenet of the particular organization. This is not always helpful, for religion is one of the aspects of life where the feelings are closely concerned, and where they can so easily override the facts.

The psychic realm has its own laws, and not all of what is perceived by psychic perception will agree with the dogmatic statements of religous organizations. whether the psychic is wrong in his observations, which is always possible, or whether the dogma of the organization needs expansion of restatement, or whether the discrepancy springs from both causes, the net result may well be quite a lot of trouble for the psychic whose findings do not agree with the religious organization concerned. For this reason, it is my own personal opinion that these things should be studied in a neutral manner, and should not be resorted to in order to support the claims of any one religious sect.

However, to essay this development under the aegis of a religious organization does bring in the question of moral issues, and it is here that the religion can enable the psychic to direct his research into such channels that he may be the better able to serve God and his fellow man.

INDEX

By the same author . . .

THE MAGICIAN:
HIS TRAINING AND WORK

The aim of the genuine magician, says W. E. Butler, is to realize that 'True Self' of which his earthly personality is but the mask.

In this book is to be found a remarkably concise explanation of the ancient uses, ritual and true aims of Magic. The author sweeps away the confusion caused by the many misconceptions, and surveys the history of Magic from the 'old religion' of pre-Christian times through to the discoveries of modern psychology. And it is, he says, with the modern school of psychology, particularly Jungian, that the magician finds his closest link with modern thought.

Since the author is writing for Western man he is not concerned with Eastern magical systems, but here explains the 'Western Tradition' of Magic. This tradition embodies the teaching and practices that have been handed down from antiquity, the central philosophy on which it hinges being the corpus of Hebrew mystical wisdom known as the Qabalah.

Written by one of the most respected occultists of the twentieth century, this manual covers every aspect of magical training, including visualization, vestments, Tattvic tides, ritual talismanic magic, the Body of Light, and the way of magical attainment.

APPRENTICED TO MAGIC
and
MAGIC AND THE QABALAH

W. E. Butler, a devoted friend and colleague of Dion Fortune, was among those who helped build the Society of the Inner Light into the foremost Mystery School of its day, before going on to found the Servants of the Light School in the late 1960s. In this special compilation volume, two of Butler's seminal works are reprinted with a new introduction by Dolores Ashcroft-Nowicki, S.O.L.'s current Director of Studies, cementing his reputation as 'The Grand Maistre of English Occultism'.

APPRENTICED TO MAGIC, designed to liberate the latent magical powers we all possess, takes the form of a series of personal instructions from a *guru* to his *chela*. The lessons are basic exercises in meditation and the training of one's visualizing power and includes information on mental exercises, magical rites and ceremonies, astral projection and the ancient Tree of Life.

MAGIC AND THE QABALAH is a stimulating examination of the QBL (literally 'from mouth to ear') and the significance of this unwritten tradition of esoteric knowledge of many centuries. The illuminating work provides much food for meditation and will be helpful in producing those changes of consciousness which are the goals of magical art.

Together the two provide the reader with an exhilarating contact with the mind of an esoteric craftsman, an inestimable privilege for anyone who aspires to initiation into Western magical practice. And if his advice is read properly, meditated upon, and followed up, it will bring those who are ready to the Doors of the Mysteries.